AMENDMENTS TO THE UNITED STATES CONSTITUTION
THE BILL OF RIGHTS

FREEDOM OF SPEECH, THE PRESS, AND RELIGION

MOLLY JONES

rosen publishing's
rosen
central®

New York

THE FIRST AMENDMENT

Published in 2011 by The Rosen Publishing Group, Inc.
29 East 21st Street, New York, NY 10010

First Edition

Library of Congress Cataloging-in-Publication Data

Jones, Molly, 1933–
The first amendment: freedom of speech, the press, and religion / Molly Jones. — 1st ed.
    p. cm. — (Amendments to the United States Constitution: the Bill of Rights)
Includes bibliographical references and index.
ISBN 978-1-4488-1252-3 (library binding)
ISBN 978-1-4488-2302-4 (pbk.)
ISBN 978-1-4488-2314-7 (6-pack)
1. United States. Constitution. 1st Amendment. 2. Freedom of expression—United States. 3. Freedom of religion—United States. 4. Petition, Right of—United States. I. Title.
KF45581st .J66 2011
342.7308'5—dc22

2010023234

Manufactured in the United States of America

CPSIA Compliance Information: Batch #W11YA: For further information, contact Rosen Publishing, New York, New York, at 1-800-237-9932.

On the cover: Left: Supporters of plans to build an Islamic cultural center near Ground Zero hold a rally in 2010. Center: A free speech supporter and Marilyn Manson fan gets his message across at a rally against the controversial artist. Right: Students demonstrate outside the U.S. Supreme Court in 2007 to support free speech rights in U.S. high schools.

CONTENTS

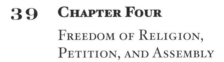
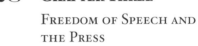

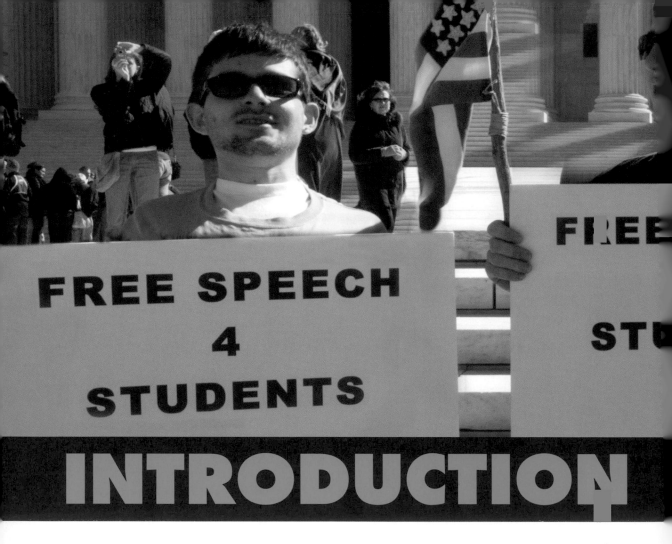

FREE SPEECH 4 STUDENTS

INTRODUCTION

On February 17, 2003, Bretton Barber was scheduled to present a compare-and-contrast essay in English class. Barber, a high school junior in Dearborn, Michigan, had decided to compare and contrast President George W. Bush with Saddam Hussein. For his presentation, he wore a T-shirt depicting the face of Bush. Near the face were the words "International Terrorist."

When Barber was in the lunchroom, the assistant principal ordered him to remove the shirt, turn the T-shirt inside out, or call his father. Barber called his father and went home.

Barber had a deep interest in the U.S. Constitution, the Bill of Rights, and the individual rights guaranteed to American citizens.

Maryland students demonstrate to support student rights in 2007. While students have the right to free speech, principals may restrict speech that disrupts the educational program.

Among the rights are those stated in the First Amendment to the Constitution:

> Congress shall make no law respecting an establishment of religion, or prohibiting the free exercise thereof; or abridging the freedom of speech, or of the press; or the right of the people peaceably to assemble, and to petition the Government for a redress of grievances.

Based on what he had learned, Barber believed that wearing his T-shirt to express his antiwar views was a form of speech protected by

Bretton Barber of Dearborn Heights, Michigan, was sent home for wearing this antiwar T-shirt to school in 2003. The ACLU fought for Barber's First Amendment right to wear the shirt and won.

the First Amendment. He also believed that Americans should defend their basic rights whenever those rights are threatened. In seventh grade, he had joined the American Civil Liberties Union (ACLU), an organization devoted to helping citizens defend their personal freedoms.

At home, Barber spoke to his high school principal on the telephone to discuss the situation. The principal insisted that the shirt was inappropriate and could not be worn in school. When Barber realized that the principal's knowledge of the law was inaccurate and that she would not consider changing the school's position, he sought help from his local ACLU chapter. On Barber's behalf, an ACLU attorney filed a lawsuit against the Dearborn public school system for violating his First Amendment rights.

In court, the principal explained her fear that Barber's T-shirt might cause a disruption, or even an outbreak of violence, among the students. However, the district court judge noted no evidence of disruption to warrant denying Barber the right to wear his T-shirt. As a result, the judge ruled that the school system had violated Barber's First Amendment rights to express his political views.

When Barber's rights were denied, the laws, organizations, and courts of the United States were ready to protect and restore those rights. In many countries, however, civil liberties don't exist. In fact, civil liberties haven't always existed for Americans. The fight has been long and hard to secure individual freedoms in the United States. Still, not everyone agrees on what freedoms and how much freedom citizens should have.

Are you free to say anything you like, whether or not what you say is true? Are newspapers and television channels free to print or display anything they like? Are citizens always free to criticize their government or request changes? Can students be required to pledge allegiance to the flag or participate in school prayers?

Protecting First Amendment rights requires every citizen to understand what those rights mean and how they were won, and to exercise vigilance, as Bretton Barber did, to protect them.

CHAPTER ONE

WHEN SPEECH WAS NOT FREE

The pioneering colonists who set out on the treacherous voyage to America left their homelands for many reasons. Some came for adventure, some to escape debt or prison, and some to make their fortunes. Many, though, set out to escape the unyielding tyranny in which their lives had been trapped.

The Tyranny Left Behind

The England that the colonists had left behind was marred by cruel tyranny. The ruling monarch ordered imprisonments and vicious beheadings for any sort of political threat, or even for personal reasons. Also, many lives were jeopardized or lost because of religious intolerance.

Religious Persecution in Europe

From the sixteenth century through the eighteenth century, there were bitter struggles in Europe between Roman Catholics, Protestants, and other religious denominations. At that time, it was believed that everyone in a society should follow the same religion. Those in power had the duty to enforce the one true faith with force, if necessary.

For example, during the reign of Edward VI from 1547 to 1553, Protestantism became the faith of the Church of England. After the

Two sixteenth-century Anglican bishops are burned at the stake for professing Protestant beliefs. Such religious intolerance drove many colonists to leave England for America.

death of Edward VI, Mary I took his place on the English throne. She was Roman Catholic and tried to undo the religious changes. She arrested and executed many Protestant leaders. John Rogers, a Catholic priest who converted to Protestantism, was the first to be killed. Rogers was burned alive in 1555. Nearly three hundred others were also executed as heretics.

Later, the Church of England again became Protestant. Brian Cansfield, a Jesuit Catholic priest, was seized while praying by the English Protestant authorities and then beaten and imprisoned. He died in 1643 as a result of his harsh treatment. The English government executed Ralph Corbington, another Jesuit priest, by hanging in 1644.

Suppression of Political Speech and Writing

In the sixteenth and seventeenth centuries, criticism of the English government or government figures was a punishable crime. Making statements that undermined the government was known as seditious libel. During this period, many people were tried for seditious libel. Government officials searched homes and offices and arrested anyone who was even suspected of libel. Officials used searches to intimidate citizens, even when evidence was not sufficient to justify an arrest.

When people were tried for seditious libel, they were found guilty if they had spoken the offending words, whether or not the words were true, and regardless of the intent. The English Bill of Rights of 1689 granted free speech to the members of Parliament, but not to ordinary citizens. They remained victims of the whims of the government.

In seventeenth-century England, books and papers had to be licensed by the government before they could be printed. Only documents that supported or were neutral to the monarch and government could be published. Harsh penalties resulted when any press or publication offended the government. Presses might be smashed, printing licenses revoked, fines issued, and physical attacks or jail sentences received by offending editors or writers.

After 1694, licensing laws and publication controls loosened. In the 1700s, there was less censorship of materials prior to publication. However, members of the press were still punished after they printed anything considered offensive, dangerous, or disruptive to peace and order.

When the early settlers left England, peaceful democratic elections were not known there. Political opponents were often executed to secure the power of the monarchy. Even the wives of monarchs might be beheaded when their existence became a problem, or simply a nuisance, for the king.

When the courageous settlers sailed away from the tyranny in England, they hoped to find a world where they could freely speak their minds, publish what they chose, worship God in their own way, and live peaceably without fear. However, they soon discovered that the freedoms they dreamed of would not be easy to obtain.

Religious Persecution Follows to the New World

England was often in religious upheaval. In the Church of England, or Anglican Church, the British monarchs could appoint themselves head of the church while also being the head of state. Regardless of who wore the English crown, the government and the church were closely tied.

Government in the new colonies was inconsistent, depending on the monarch in power. Often, the tyranny the colonists had tried to escape seemed to have followed them.

Protestant groups that had broken off from the Anglican Church were among those that set out for a New World where they could worship freely. For example, the Quakers, Protestants who believed that every person could find God and salvation on his or her own, ventured

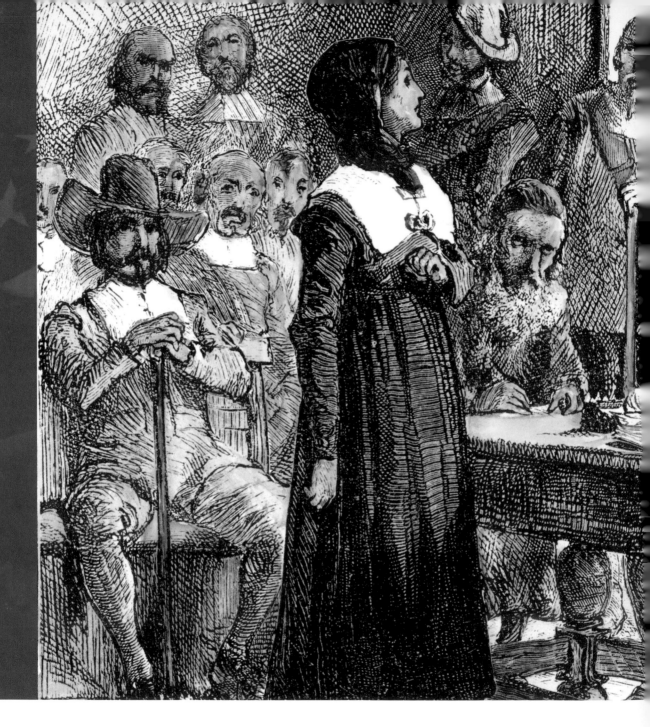

to the New World for religious freedom. Another group, the Puritans,
wanted to rid the church of corruption and wrongful teachings. Often
persecuted by Anglicans in England, they settled in Massachusetts with
the intent of creating "a city of God on Earth."

Anne Hutchinson, who came to America to escape religious intolerance in England, found the Massachusetts Puritans to be just as intolerant. Outspoken about religion, she was banished from the colony in 1638.

Unfortunately, those who came to America seeking religious freedom for themselves did not always give that freedom to others. Each group believed their religion was the one true faith that everyone should follow. For example, once established, the Puritans in America were as intolerant of other religious groups as the Anglicans in England had been of them. Cruel punishments for religious nonconformity were as common in the colonies as they had been in England and Europe. Quakers in Puritan Massachusetts risked banishment, physical punishment, and even execution.

Similarly, Governor Peter Stuyvesant of the Dutch colony of New Netherland, later named New York, banned all religions except the Dutch Reformed Church. In 1657, Stuyvesant ordered the public torture of a twenty-three-year-old Quaker preacher, Robert Hodgson. Anyone protecting Quakers in the colony was subject to a fine and imprisonment.

Preaching against Puritan beliefs in the Massachusetts Colony was unacceptable; a woman daring to oppose the teachings of her male spiritual leader was unthinkable. The daughter of a clergyman, Anne Hutchinson spent her early life trying to understand the beliefs, corruption, and political motivations of the leaders of the Anglican Church. After escaping to the colonies, she encountered the religious tyranny of the Puritans in Massachusetts. She emphasized personal religion and invited women and men to meetings in her home to discuss the Sunday sermons. She began to attract a large following. Though she had come to America to worship as she saw fit, speaking openly about her beliefs in America brought only denouncement by the governor of Massachusetts, John Winthrop. Hutchinson was tried in 1637 and banished from the community in 1638.

Witch Trials Punish Nonconformists

Puritans in England and America believed that witchcraft was a method used by the Devil to spread evil. In the 1690s, witchcraft was a major crime punishable by death in Massachusetts. If someone accused another of "afflicting" or casting an evil spell upon him or her, the accused person could be arrested, tried, and punished with imprisonment or execution.

In 1692, in Salem, Massachusetts, several young girls began to show unusual behaviors, including making strange sounds, complaining of feeling pinpricks, and twisting themselves into strange positions. They accused three women, including a slave named Tituba, of afflicting them. Soon, hysteria about witchcraft spread. Eventually, dozens of women and a few men were accused of practicing witchcraft. More than 150 people, mostly single women and other people who seemed "different," were imprisoned. About thirty people were tried and convicted. Nineteen of the accused were hanged, and another was crushed under heavy stones. At least five died in prison. Those who argued for their rights and denied practicing witchcraft were the most likely to be punished severely.

Since none of the accused had actually injured anyone, this treatment was a cruel form of religious and social persecution. A new royal governor ended the witchcraft court and set the remaining prisoners free. The episode of the witch trials eventually led to the decline of Puritanism in Massachusetts.

In many of the other colonies, a single denomination was established as the official religion. For example, laws in Jamestown, Virginia, established the Anglican Church as the official religion in the colony. Congregationalism was established in Connecticut and in most of the other New England colonies.

Taxpayers were required to support the official church, regardless of their personal beliefs. Ministers and members of other religions could face beatings, stonings, and jail sentences.

A Fettered Press Keeps Liberty at Bay

In 1690, a century before the Bill of Rights established freedom of the press in America, Benjamin Harris published the first American newspaper, *Publick Occurrences*, in Boston, Massachusetts. Harris wanted to present facts and opinions about the issues of the day. However, according to British law, publishing without the approval of the government was illegal. Four days after *Publick Occurrences* was published, the British-appointed

Benjamin Harris published the first American newspaper, *Publick Occurrences*, to present facts about current issues. The British government immediately banned the paper.

governor and council banned the newspaper. They ordered that future publications, including pamphlets and reports of all kinds, would have to be licensed by the government.

Almost one hundred years later, in 1787, Thomas Jefferson would write, "Were it left to me to decide whether we should have a government without newspapers or newspapers without a government, I should not hesitate a moment to prefer the latter."

Not everyone would have agreed with Jefferson, especially in the early years of the colonies. In 1671, Governor William Berkeley of Virginia wrote:

> I thank God there are no free schools or printing; and I hope we shall not have [them] these hundred years; for learning has brought disobedience and heresy, and sects into the world, and printing has divulged them, and libels against the government. God keep us from both!

Clearly, some colonial leaders valued peace and calm more than the freedom to share disturbing facts and information with the public.

The Zenger Case

Like Benjamin Harris, a German immigrant printer named John Peter Zenger was willing to risk expressing his views, even in a time of tight government control over the press.

In November 1733, Zenger published the first issue of the *New York Weekly Journal*. The newspaper aimed to publicize the truth about the actions of the British-appointed governor, William Cosby. (The other newspaper in New York had strong ties to the governor and published only flattering stories about him.) After several months of enduring

John Peter Zenger's newspaper is burned in 1734 because his writings criticized the governor of New York. Zenger was initially jailed. But after his trial, the court upheld his right to publish the complaints.

criticism, Cosby attempted to shut down the newspaper by accusing Zenger of seditious libel. Zenger was arrested, and after ten months in jail, he was tried in 1735.

In the court battle, Zenger's lawyer admitted that Zenger published writings that criticized the governor. However, he argued that people in the colonies should have the right to publish complaints about abuses of power. Sympathetic to the idea of free speech, the jury members declared Zenger not guilty.

In all, at least 1,244 seditious press and speech prosecutions were recorded in colonial times. Zenger's trial was a major step in rousing the public's opposition to government suppression of the press.

CHAPTER TWO

THE FIGHT FOR A BILL OF RIGHTS

The early 1770s saw a growing spirit of independence in the American colonies. Eventually, the mounting abuses of British colonial rule brought about a massive revolt, and the colonies declared their independence from England in 1776. Though the Revolutionary War resulted in the political freedom of the American states, a broad challenge still lay ahead to build a nation free of the tyranny the colonists had sought to escape. The Americans found that creating a land of freedom would not be free or easy. Their first task was to create a governing plan under which the thirteen separate and autonomous colonies could work together.

The American Colonies Break Free

In 1774, before the Revolutionary War, the colonies sent fifty-four delegates to the First Continental Congress in Philadelphia, Pennsylvania. The delegates formed an association to cooperate in trade, business, defense, and dealings with the British government. The congress prepared a declaration stating that Britain was depriving the colonists of their rights as Englishmen. Specifically, they objected to thirteen acts passed by Parliament that had come to be known as the Intolerable Acts. In their declaration, the congress included a listing of rights and pledged to boycott all trade with Britain until the acts were repealed. The disputes with Britain were not resolved, and in 1775, the congress met again to prepare for war with England.

In 1776, the Second Continental Congress convened in Philadelphia. This congress adopted the Declaration of Independence. This document announced the separation of the colonies from Great Britain and explained the reasons for the American Revolution. It began with the bold proclamation that "all men are created equal, that they are endowed by their Creator with certain unalienable Rights, that among these are Life, Liberty and the pursuit of Happiness." Meanwhile, each state began to forge its own constitution and state government. Some states, such as Virginia, created documents guaranteeing citizens' individual rights.

During the Revolutionary War, the Continental Congress wrote the Articles of Confederation. The Articles of Confederation established a national government under which the states agreed to cooperate. After ratification by all thirteen states, the articles became law in 1781. Under the Articles of Confederation, the main functions of government, including the protection of individual rights, were placed in the hands of the separate states. In time, many leaders came to believe that a stronger central government was needed, one with power to levy taxes, take actions in defense of the whole, and deal with issues such as trade and currency.

Forging a New Kind of Government

Emotions ran high as state leaders and ordinary citizens began to discuss forming a stronger union of states and a stronger central government.

In May 1787, the Philadelphia Constitutional Convention met in order to amend (change and improve) the Articles of Confederation. However, the result proposed by the convention was an entirely new constitution. The plan was based largely on a model of government submitted by the Virginia delegation, led by James Madison. Two areas of controversy that divided the delegates were: (1) how power would be divided between the federal government and the states; and (2) how representatives would be apportioned in Congress, an issue that divided small and large states. After months of debate, the delegates made a series of compromises and reached agreement on the main elements of the U.S. Constitution.

Individual Rights: An Elusive Vision

The abuses of British rule were still vivid in the memories of the American people. Though the

In front of Independence Hall in Philadelphia, Pennsylvania, citizens celebrate America's independence on July 4, 2002. Participants wear costumes to depict the events that set the nation free more than two centuries ago.

Philadelphia delegates earnestly desired to create a government in which such abuses could not happen, they disagreed about how to accomplish that goal. Many delegates, including George Washington, George Mason, and Patrick Henry, wanted to include a bill of rights in the proposed constitution. The bill of rights would directly state the rights and freedoms that would belong to the people. Mason felt so strongly about this that he declared he would not vote to ratify a constitution that did not include a bill of rights.

Others believed such a statement of rights was unnecessary. Most states already had bills of rights in their constitutions, and some delegates believed that these were sufficient. Some argued that the federal

George Washington addresses delegates to the Constitutional Convention in Philadelphia, Pennsylvania, in 1787. A widely respected leader and general, Washington was the overwhelming choice to be the nation's first president.

government would have no powers except those granted to it by the U.S. Constitution. Therefore, individual rights would automatically be protected, since the government would have no power to deny them.

Other opponents to a bill of rights claimed that stating a specific set of rights could actually limit individual rights. Such a list, they argued, would imply that citizens could not claim any rights that were not on the list.

Madison and the other delegates eventually worked out a plan so that the convention could move forward. Those who insisted on including a bill of rights agreed to vote for the proposed constitution, provided that the new Congress would immediately adopt amendments that added the rights in question. Thus in accord, on September 17, 1787, the members of the Philadelphia Convention signed the U.S. Constitution.

The Ratification Battle

When the completed Constitution was sent to the states for ratification, there was a great deal of controversy. Some people favored adoption of the new Constitution, but others were strongly opposed.

Those in favor of ratification, known as Federalists, favored a strong central government. James Madison worked tirelessly for months during and after the convention to convince Americans that a strong national government would be in the best interests of all. Madison, Alexander Hamilton, and John Jay wrote a series of letters to newspapers that became known as the Federalist Papers, explaining their arguments for ratification.

However, other citizens and leaders, known as Anti-Federalists, believed the states should not give up so much of their power to a central government. Also, they were not convinced that individual rights would be adequately protected. They feared that a strong federal government would lead to tyranny. Well-known Anti-Federalists included Patrick Henry, George Mason, and Samuel Adams.

Federalists believed it was especially important that Virginia ratify the Constitution. George Washington, a Virginia native, was widely expected to be the first president. He and other prominent Virginia leaders would not be eligible to hold office in the new government unless Virginia came into the union.

Patrick Henry and other Anti-Federalists were determined to defeat the Constitution. They warned their constituents that states would lose rights and power to the federal government and that individual rights would not be protected.

How a Proposed Constitutional Amendment Becomes Law

The Framers of the Constitution of the United States took care to see that changes in the nation's fundamental law could not be made hastily or unwisely. In more than two centuries, only twenty-seven amendments to the Constitution have been ratified. Article V of the Constitution specifies the steps necessary to propose and ratify an amendment:

1. *Proposal:* An amendment may be proposed by either Congress or the states. A vote of two-thirds of both houses of Congress can propose an amendment. Alternatively, the legislatures of two-thirds of the states may call a convention to propose an amendment.

2. *Ratification:* A proposed amendment will become part of the Constitution when ratified by the legislatures of three-fourths of the states.

However, by May 1790, all thirteen states had at last ratified the new Constitution. Five states ratified with reservations. Most of these states specified that their votes would be valid only if a bill of rights were promptly adopted.

The Birth of the First Amendment

By April 1, 1789, enough members of the new Congress had arrived in New York City, the first capital of the nation, to conduct business. A host of urgent tasks lay ahead. One of the most urgent was to initiate the process of securing individual rights for all citizens.

Many Anti-Federalists, such as Patrick Henry, had demanded that another Constitutional Convention be called. This convention would draft a bill of rights. It would also work to limit the powers of the federal government and protect states' autonomy and power.

James Madison and other Federalists opposed the idea of a second convention. They feared that the ideas proposed by Anti-Federalists would undermine the hard-won compromises and balances of power the first Constitutional Convention had achieved. Instead, Madison took it upon himself to draft a set of proposed constitutional amendments for the new legislators to consider.

Several earlier English documents provided models for Madison in writing these amendments. The Magna Carta, accepted by King John in 1215, did not grant individual rights to all citizens. However, it did provide an example of a sovereign being required to work within the law. The English Bill of Rights, adopted in 1689, went a step further in ending the absolute rule of the British monarchy. This document established the right of Parliament to control some functions of government. In America, the state of Virginia adopted a Declaration of Rights in 1776, guaranteeing individual rights such as freedom of speech and religion.

Federal Hall in New York City was the first capitol building of the United States. Here, George Washington was inaugurated president, and the Bill of Rights was ratified.

Working from these precedents, Madison drafted a set of amendments. He presented them to the full House on August 13, 1789. On August 24, the House forwarded seventeen approved amendments to the Senate.

In the Senate, after removing one amendment and rewording and combining others, twelve amendments were approved. A conference committee was appointed to reconcile the House and Senate amendments. Three days later, the nation's Bill of Rights had passed Congress.

Finally, the amendments were sent to the individual states for approval, the last step in amending the Constitution. In December 1791, enough states ratified the Bill of Rights to make it the law of the land. On March 1, 1792, almost three years after the first Congress was called to order, Secretary of State Thomas Jefferson announced that the Bill of Rights was officially part of the Constitution.

Ratification did not answer the question of whether these rights, guaranteed by the federal government, had to be observed by state governments as well. The question was widely debated. In 1868, the Fourteenth Amendment to the Constitution finally mandated that both state governments and the federal government had to abide by the protections of the Bill of Rights.

CHAPTER THREE

FREEDOM OF SPEECH AND THE PRESS

Each of the first ten amendments has distinctly influenced the course of American history, but none more than the First Amendment. The protection the First Amendment guarantees for freedom of speech and freedom of the press gives essential support to other rights and freedoms. In protecting free expression, the First Amendment empowers the people and limits the control of the government.

Early Implementation

Believe it or not, for well over one hundred years after the ratification of the Bill of Rights, the First Amendment attracted little attention. At

Women protest the imprisonment of family members under the Espionage Act of 1917 and the Sedition Act of 1918. Despite the First Amendment, the laws criminalized speech that was critical of the government.

times, officials simply ignored the First Amendment when its requirements were inconvenient, such as when the government wanted to stifle critical speech in wartime.

Only seven years after the Bill of Rights became law, President John Adams signed the Sedition Act of 1798. This law made it a criminal act to speak or write maliciously about the president or Congress. Defenders of the First Amendment protested the act, which they said stifled political discussion. The act expired two years later and was not renewed.

During the Civil War, President Abraham Lincoln allowed the jailing of thirteen thousand civilians who were suspected of aiding the

Confederacy. Some of their offenses included discouraging people from volunteering for the draft and criticizing the president's policies.

A few decades later, under the Espionage Act of 1917, more than two thousand prosecutions involving antigovernment speech took place. Several individuals were convicted for publishing a pamphlet of writing that opposed the draft, sympathized with Germany, and favored socialism. The Sedition Act of 1918 criminalized any disloyal or abusive language about the government.

In recent decades, however, numerous legal cases have begun to unleash the power and test the limits of each of the First Amendment's five components.

The Scope and Limits of Free Speech

Are there ever times when free speech can be restricted? Throughout the twentieth century and into the twenty-first, the words drafted by Madison and his colleagues, "Congress shall make no law . . . abridging the freedom of speech," have been pressed into service in situations the authors could not have imagined.

The Cornell Law Institute lists well over one hundred cases heard by the U.S. Supreme Court, beginning in 1919, in which the freedom of speech clause of the First Amendment has been relevant. A sample of these cases illustrates the range of activities the court has interpreted as "speech." The cases also show some important principles that have evolved to test the limits of free speech.

In 1919, Charles Schenck, who had sent leaflets to recently drafted men opposing military conscription, was convicted of violating the Espionage Act. Schenck challenged his conviction based on the free speech clause of the First Amendment. However, the Supreme Court, in

In 1919, Supreme Court Justice Oliver Wendell Holmes Jr. articulated the phrase "a clear and present danger," which became an important measure for testing the limits of free speech.

Charles T. Schenck v. United States, upheld the conviction. Justice Oliver Wendell Holmes Jr. stated, "The question in every case is whether the words are used in such circumstances and are of such a nature as to create a clear and present danger." Holmes argued that while free speech must be protected, there must be limits on speech in certain circumstances. He said, "The most stringent protection of free speech would not protect a man in falsely shouting fire in a theater and causing a panic." In this case, the "danger" was the possibility that Schenck's words might interfere with the draft or weaken the obedience of soldiers in a time of war.

Holmes's criterion, "a clear and present danger," was applied in later cases involving antigovernment or antiwar speech. In 1940, the Smith Act made it illegal to advocate the overthrow of the U.S. government by force or violence, or to organize a group of people who advocate this. The Supreme Court ruled in 1951 that the law was constitutional (in accordance with the Constitution and the Bill of Rights). However, in *Yates v. United States* (1957), the Court distinguished between speaking about the idea of overthrowing the government, which does not pose a clear and present danger, and inciting violent actions to carry out an overthrow, which does pose such a danger.

Antiwar demonstrators burn their draft cards on the steps of the Pentagon in Washington, D.C., during the Vietnam War. The Supreme Court ruled that draft card burning was a crime.

Many activities have been considered "speech" in First Amendment cases. Examples include words and images printed on clothing, flag burning, refusal to salute the flag, contributing to political campaigns, nudity and profane expletives on TV, and displaying symbols of hate. In

the 1968 case *United States v. O'Brien*, a law prohibiting the destruction of draft cards was ruled constitutional because the action could interfere with the draft.

On the other hand, the right to wear symbols or printed words denouncing the draft was upheld in a number of cases. Similarly, freedom to mutilate the American flag has been upheld because such an action does not pose any "clear and present danger" to the nation. In the case *Texas v. Johnson* (1989), flag burning was determined to be protected political speech, even if society might find it offensive.

In cases involving the speech of hate groups, the Supreme Court has distinguished between speech that expresses ideas, opinions, or personal values, and speech that threatens harm or intimidates a person or group. For example, in 1977, the Court ruled that members of the Nazi Party of America were permitted to march in the streets of Skokie, Illinois, and express their views as long as they marched peacefully and physical threats were not involved.

Making deliberately false statements that harm the reputation of a person or group is not protected under the First Amendment. This kind of speech is called slander when it is spoken and libel when it is written. Victims of slander or libel can sue for money to compensate for the harm to their personal lives and businesses.

In addition, the First Amendment does not protect obscene materials as free speech. However, it has been a challenge for the courts to define what is and what isn't obscene for adults to listen to or view. According to the Supreme Court decision in *Miller v. California* (1973), if a book, magazine, movie, or other material can be judged to have serious literary, artistic, political, or scientific value, it is not obscene. It is therefore protected by the First Amendment.

In order to protect children from harm or abuse, the Court has said there can be laws restricting what materials are sold or distributed to juveniles. There are also restrictions on the kinds of materials in which children can appear. Similarly, schools have been allowed to restrict materials used on computers inside schools. Whether or not material presents a "clear and present danger" to those affected may determine if it is protected as free speech.

The Press Challenges Its Boundaries

The First Amendment states that "Congress shall make no law . . . abridging the freedom of the press." But are there ever times when the government can and should restrict what the press prints?

Long before the First Amendment was ratified, John Peter Zenger had successfully challenged government attempts to control the press. Once freedom of the press became part of the Constitution, questions began to arise about what this meant. Each case added new complexities to the meaning and limits of freedom.

Freedom from Prior Restraint

The First Amendment protects the press from "prior restraint" by the government. In other words, the government cannot censor or prevent the publication of a document, broadcast, or other material. Publication of information can only be stopped in exceptional cases. For example, prior restraint may be permitted in order to prevent severe and immediate damage to national security.

This principle was tested in 1979 when an antinuclear activist, Howard Morland, wrote an article describing the "secret" of making an H-bomb. An injunction was issued to prevent publication of the article. However, Morland showed that he had obtained his information from sources freely available to the public. Consequently, the government dropped its case.

The First Amendment in Action

Hundreds of times, the First Amendment has been put to the test. For example, an important challenge to freedom of the press occurred in 1971.

The Supreme Court case: New York Times Co. v. United States. In 1971, the federal government attempted to block the *New York Times* from publishing a report that revealed internal government strategies leading up to the Vietnam War. The report, known as the *Pentagon Papers*, had been classified. In other words, only authorized persons were allowed to read it.

The government's argument: Publication of the report could be a threat to national security.

The newspaper's argument: While publication of the report would reveal prewar government strategy that had been kept secret from the public, it would not reveal information that threatened security.

The outcome: After a lengthy trial, the Supreme Court ruled in favor of the *New York Times*. The court stated that blocking publication, or prior restraint, was a serious form of censorship. It was justified only when the government could show, beyond a doubt, that publication would endanger national security. In this case, while publication may have been an embarrassment to the government, the Court believed it did not threaten national security.

Daniel Ellsberg reads about his trial before a California court in 1973. Ellsberg's *New York Times* article revealed activities the government wanted to keep secret.

Shield Laws

News reporters sometimes obtain important information from confidential sources. When the matter involves a crime or other circumstance important to the government, the court sometimes subpoenas (legally summons) reporters to testify and reveal their sources. Also, reporters are sometimes asked to share their notes or other unpublished information related to a story.

Though some people believe that subpoenas should override freedom of the press, others believe that involving reporters in legal cases is damaging to journalism. Many journalists argue that if they break a promise of confidentiality to a source, other sources will not trust them in the future. This may prevent reporters from getting the information they need about a story and bringing that information to the public. In a number of cases, journalists have gone to jail, rather than obey a court's order to reveal their sources.

In response, some states have passed shield laws. A shield law protects a reporter from being forced to reveal confidential sources, provide information, or testify. Currently, there is no national shield law.

Limits on Broadcasting

In the fifteenth century, the printing press presented a major threat to the power of authorities, both governmental and religious. Suddenly, information and ideas could be spread widely among ordinary people who had previously accepted authority without question. Today, not only the press, but also radio, television, computers, telephones, and other devices enable people to communicate rapidly worldwide. As a result, the freedom of the press clause of the First Amendment has been stretched to cover a wide range of situations. In every new case, the courts must seek a balance between the protection of freedom and the avoidance of harm to some segment of the population.

The Fairness Doctrine and the Equal Time Rule have historically limited the freedom of broadcasters. The Fairness Doctrine, which was made part of Federal Communications Commission (FCC) regulations in 1967, required licensed broadcasters to present important controversial issues in an honest, equitable, and balanced way. In 1987, the Fairness Doctrine was abolished because it was deemed to violate the First Amendment guarantee of free speech. Some have tried to reinstate the doctrine, but support has not been adequate.

The Equal Time Rule, found in both the Radio Act of 1927 and the Communications Act of 1934, requires radio and television stations to treat qualified political candidates equally in their programming when giving away or selling airtime. The act also prohibits a station from censoring what a candidate says.

The FCC has been given authority to regulate indecency, such as indecent bodily exposure or vulgar language, on television and radio. The Supreme Court has said the government should have the power to regulate broadcast media, since it is present in every part of our lives and is "uniquely accessible to children." In the case *FCC v. Pacifica Foundation* (1978), the Court ruled that the FCC could restrict the times when indecent language is broadcast to hours when children are not likely to be listening. A 2001 case updated the guidelines to distinguish between cable channels and regular broadcast media. The Court said that since cable channels can be chosen or blocked by individual households, regulation by the government is not necessary.

CHAPTER FOUR

FREEDOM OF RELIGION, PETITION, AND ASSEMBLY

A merica's founders included men and women willing to protest, challenge, and even sacrifice their lives for the freedoms they had come to the New World to find. Those courageous Americans would not simply accept assurances that their rights would be respected. They demanded freedom of religion and a guarantee of access to the government in order to address their elected leaders.

Religious Freedom: An Ongoing Discussion

The quest for religious freedom brought many of the colonists to the New World, and the First Amendment finally embodied their dream.

There are two phrases in the First Amendment that discuss religious freedom. The First Amendment states, "Congress shall make no law respecting an establishment of religion, or prohibiting the free exercise thereof." The first phrase, known as the Establishment Clause, protects citizens from a government-required or government-supported religion. The second phrase is known as the Free Exercise Clause; it protects citizens from government interference in their practice of religion.

However, acting to uphold one of these principles can put the government in conflict with the other. For example, not allowing a religious group to use a public area may prevent the government from being viewed as supporting a particular religion. At the same time, it may discriminate against a group of citizens who want to express their religious beliefs in a public place.

Conflicts also arise when the religious practice of a person or group interferes with the freedoms and rights of others. In the 1980s, a group of Native Americans challenged the U.S. Forest Service's plan to build a logging road in a national forest and log an area near Chimney Rock, one of their sacred places. The Forest Service did intend to protect the parts of the area that the Native Americans used. In a suit against

A marker displays the Ten Commandments outside of Peebles High School in Peebles, Ohio, in 2002. In accordance with the Establishment Clause of the First Amendment, the marker was removed.

the Forest Service, *Northwest Indian Cemetery Protective Association v. Peterson*, the Native Americans claimed that, despite the protection, the road building and logging would destroy the privacy, solitude, and undisturbed natural setting necessary for their religious practice. As a result,

they argued, it violated their First Amendment right to freely exercise their religion.

Many groups sympathized with the Native Americans, and they succeeding in stopping the Forest Service in lower courts. However, in *Lyng v. Northwest Indian Cemetery Protective Association*, the Supreme Court rejected their claim and ruled that the Forest Service could do the construction and timber harvesting. The Court argued that reserving public land for the sole use of a specific group would open the door for other religious groups to interfere with the use of public land all over the United States.

Since the government operates public schools, rulings based on the Establishment Clause have prohibited religious instruction, religious displays, and required religious activities or school-sponsored prayer in public schools. While educators may not lead prayers, students have the right to pray voluntarily on school grounds.

After many cases and extensive debate, several principles have evolved for evaluating cases involving government and religion. A government law or action must have a nonreligious purpose and must not excessively entangle or involve the government in religion. The action must neither advance nor inhibit any religion. In short, government must take a neutral position on religion, treating religious groups as they treat other groups.

Roger Williams, the Baptist founder of the Rhode Island Colony, first used the term "wall of separation" in 1644. Today, the phrase "separation of church and state" continues to describe the boundary line that must be maintained when government and religion interact.

Assembly and Petition: The People's Right to Challenge the Government

In the twenty-first century, Americans expect more than ever to have a voice in their government. The assembly and petition clauses of the First

Amendment state, "Congress shall make no law ... abridging ... the right of the people to peaceably assemble, and to petition the Government for a redress of grievances." These words are just as relevant in today's political climate as they were in the 1700s. The power of group action and direct petition of government continues to enable citizens to influence their leaders.

Freedom of Petition

Americans did not always have the right to petition those in power. In the 1770s, King George III was indifferent to the pleas of the colonists. After enumerating the wrongs they had endured without relief, American leaders saw no solution but to revolt. In the Declaration of Independence, Thomas Jefferson wrote, "In every stage of these oppressions, we have petitioned for redress, in the most humble terms; our repeated petitions have been answered only by repeated injury."

Those who pushed for the Bill of Rights were determined that the new government be responsive to public concerns. Therefore, the First Amendment included a guarantee that the people's petitions would be received. (In fact, the initial draft of the First Amendment contained only the petition and assembly clauses.)

While the right to address government officials is guaranteed, nothing in the First Amendment guarantees that officials will listen or respond. Still, keeping an open channel of communication from citizens to their government keeps officials aware of the public's opinions and needs. Petitions and protests may also alert officials to any negative effects of government policies.

For the colonists, the rights to assemble and petition meant the ability to gather and distribute information, join forces for common causes, and express widely held concerns. Today, technology enables people to communicate views and information in a more rapid, widespread way than ever before. Much organizing and petitioning is done via the Internet, rapid mail delivery, broadcasting, electronic publishing, film, and other methods.

Historically, the petition clause of the First Amendment has seldom been applied to cases separately from the speech and assembly clauses. More recently, though, the right to petition has been extended to include any nonviolent, legal means of expressing approval or disapproval of government actions, such as lobbying, conducting e-mail or letter-writing campaigns, filing lawsuits, or picketing.

Freedom of Assembly

The Supreme Court has repeatedly ruled that a community cannot restrict group gatherings based on the beliefs or content discussed by group members. In general, citizens have been judged free to assemble as long as their gathering does not present a danger to the local government's ability to maintain order, protect people from physical harm, or protect the community environment from destruction. Protest groups, such as civil rights or right-to-life activists, as well as groups opposed to the government, must be allowed to assemble peacefully as long as participants observe the laws of the community.

The Supreme Court has also ruled that the government has the right to create reasonable restrictions about the "time, place, and manner" of group gatherings. For example, a community

Thousands of antiwar demonstrators fill a street near the Capitol building in Washington, D.C., in 2007. Groups that oppose government policies enjoy the same freedom of assembly that supporters enjoy.

can prevent a group from marching loudly through a quiet neighbor-hood at 3 AM or from interfering with traffic flow in the town. However, the rules have to apply to all groups equally and cannot be related to the group's message. Also, when restrictions are made, groups must be given an alternative means of assembling and expressing their views.

The Court has considered the principle of freedom of assembly when ruling on the constitutionality of curfew ordinances. In 2003, the town of Vernon, Connecticut, declared a curfew to reduce juvenile crime and victimization. However, the curfew was declared unconstitutional in *Ramos v. Town of Vernon*. The town's government argued that it created a curfew for public safety reasons, but it failed to prove that crime had been a problem during curfew hours. The Court sometimes permits restrictions on freedom of assembly when the ordinance serves an important government interest, such as youth safety. However, the restrictions must be proven necessary, and they cannot go beyond what is needed to serve the government interest. In some cases, the courts have permitted curfews if there were exceptions in the ordinances to protect other First Amendment rights.

A Work in Progress

After more than two hundred years and scores of cases examining First Amendment freedoms, precedents and criteria have gradually evolved by which new situations can be tested. However, no new situation is exactly like an earlier one, and circumstances constantly arise that don't fit into previous molds. In addition, one judge's view on how to apply the criteria may differ greatly from another judge's view. Thus, those appointed to judgeships at any given time have a powerful influence on the ways in which First Amendment freedoms are interpreted.

What Do Americans Think About the First Amendment?

The First Amendment Center, an affiliate of Vanderbilt University and the Freedom Forum, is a nonpartisan forum for the study of free expression issues. For fourteen consecutive years, the First Amendment Center has conducted an annual survey to assess American attitudes toward the First Amendment. Responses from the 2009 survey suggest that many Americans do not fully understand or appreciate the role of the First Amendment in protecting their freedoms.

- When asked to identify any of the freedoms guaranteed by the First Amendment, more than one in three could not name a single one of the freedoms.

- More than one in five people surveyed believe the First Amendment goes too far in the rights it guarantees to citizens.

- Almost one in three people surveyed believe musicians should not be allowed to sing songs that others might find offensive.

- More than one-third of respondents said the press has too much freedom to do what it wants.

- At the same time, seven in ten Americans believe it is important for the media to act as a watchdog of the government.

If Americans want an open government, rather than a secretive and deceptive government, they must learn about and guard their heritage of free speech, freedom of the press, and freedoms to assemble and petition, as well as their religious freedom.

To illustrate how different Supreme Courts can issue different judgments, an opinion handed down by the Supreme Court in 2010 revealed a distinctly different view of freedom of speech from an earlier Court's ruling. In *Citizens United v. Federal Election Commission*, the 2010 Court ruled that the government cannot make laws that limit spending by corporations in political campaigns. This judgment overrode rulings in 1990 and 2003 that did allow the government to limit corporate campaign spending.

Many First Amendment questions still do not have a final answer. For example, the Court is not yet clear about the degree to which cyber speech should be controlled and when, if ever, obscenity and profanity should be censored. As America and its people change, new criteria will be needed to fit new circumstances.

The State of First Amendment Freedoms Today

Because of First Amendment freedoms, a U.S. citizen can be patriotic while opposing particular government actions. In fact, Americans can be even more strongly patriotic because they value their freedom to express opposition, question government policies, expose corruption or deception, and protest and petition for change. In some countries, citizens can be jailed and even executed for such actions.

Present generations of American citizens, unless they came to this country from a totalitarian nation, have not known a time without these freedoms. Most Americans today did not have to struggle to obtain their freedoms as earlier generations did, but were born possessing them.

The First Amendment Center points out that, without the First Amendment, the United States might be very different. It would be possible for religious minorities to be persecuted, for the government to establish a national religion, for those who disagree with the government

The Newseum, a six-level, interactive museum in Washington, D.C., traces the history of news reporting from the sixteenth century to the present. It includes exhibits that examine First Amendment freedoms.

to be silenced, and for the press to be barred from criticizing the government. Citizens might be unable to meet and mobilize for social change. Supreme Court Justice William O. Douglas has described the immeasurable value of the First Amendment. He wrote, "Restriction on free thought and free speech is the most dangerous of all subversions. It is the one un-American act that could most easily defeat us."

First Amendment freedoms will be safe, however, as long as every citizen actively guards them with watchfulness and persistence, as Bretton Barber did in his high school.

AMENDMENTS
TO THE U.S. CONSTITUTION

First Amendment (proposed 1789; ratified 1791): Freedom of religion, speech, press, assembly, and petition

Second Amendment (proposed 1789; ratified 1791): Right to bear arms

Third Amendment (proposed 1789; ratified 1791): No quartering of soldiers in private houses in times of peace

Fourth Amendment (proposed 1789; ratified 1791): Interdiction of unreasonable search and seizure; requirement of search warrants

Fifth Amendment (proposed 1789; ratified 1791): Indictments; due process; self-incrimination; double jeopardy; eminent domain

Sixth Amendment (proposed 1789; ratified 1791): Right to a fair and speedy public trial; notice of accusations; confronting one's accuser; subpoenas; right to counsel

Seventh Amendment (proposed 1789; ratified 1791): Right to a trial by jury in civil cases

Eighth Amendment (proposed 1789; ratified 1791): No excessive bail and fines; no cruel or unusual punishment

Ninth Amendment (proposed 1789; ratified 1791): Protection of unenumerated rights (rights inferred from other legal rights but that are not themselves coded or enumerated in written constitution and laws)

Tenth Amendment (proposed 1789; ratified 1791): Limits the power of the federal government

Eleventh Amendment (proposed 1794; ratified 1795): Sovereign immunity (immunity of states from suits brought by out-of-state citizens and foreigners living outside of states' borders)

Twelfth Amendment (proposed 1803; ratified 1804): Revision of presidential election procedures (electoral college)

Thirteenth Amendment (proposed 1865; ratified 1865): Abolition of slavery

Fourteenth Amendment (proposed 1866; ratified 1868): Citizenship; state due process; application of Bill of Rights to states; revision to apportionment of congressional representatives; denies public office to anyone who has rebelled against the United States

Fifteenth Amendment (proposed 1869; ratified 1870): Suffrage no longer restricted by race

Sixteenth Amendment (proposed 1909; ratified 1913): Allows federal income tax

Seventeenth Amendment (proposed 1912; ratified 1913): Direct election to the U.S. Senate by popular vote

Eighteenth Amendment (proposed 1917; ratified 1919): Prohibition of alcohol

Nineteenth Amendment (proposed 1919; ratified 1920): Women's suffrage

Twentieth Amendment (proposed 1932; ratified 1933): Term commencement for Congress (January 3) and president (January 20)

Twenty-first Amendment (proposed 1933; ratified 1933): Repeal of Eighteenth Amendment (Prohibition)

Twenty-second Amendment (proposed 1947; ratified 1951): Limits president to two terms

Twenty-third Amendment (proposed 1960; ratified 1961): Representation of D.C. in electoral college

Twenty-fourth Amendment (proposed 1962; ratified 1964): Prohibition of restriction of voting rights due to nonpayment of poll taxes

Twenty-fifth Amendment (proposed 1965; ratified 1967): Presidential succession

Twenty-sixth Amendment (proposed 1971; ratified 1971): Voting age of eighteen

Twenty-seventh Amendment (proposed 1789; ratified 1992): Congressional compensation

Proposed but Unratified Amendments

Congressional Apportionment Amendment (proposed 1789; still technically pending): Apportionment of U.S. representatives

Titles of Nobility Amendment (proposed 1810; still technically pending): Prohibition of titles of nobility

Corwin Amendment (proposed 1861; still technically pending though superseded by Thirteenth Amendment): Preservation of slavery

Child Labor Amendment (proposed 1924; still technically pending): Congressional power to regulate child labor

Equal Rights Amendment (proposed 1972; expired): Prohibition of inequality of men and women

District of Columbia Voting Rights Amendment (proposed 1978; expired): District of Columbia voting rights

GLOSSARY

ACLU American Civil Liberties Union; a nonpartisan organization devoted to helping citizens defend their personal freedoms.

acquitted Declared not guilty of an accusation or charge.

act A law or statute made official by a lawmaking body or a monarch.

amendment A new article added to the Constitution or a change in an existing article.

Anti-Federalist A person who opposed a strong national government for the United States.

article A distinct section of a writing, such as in the Constitution.

assembly A grouping together of people for a common purpose.

bill A proposed law, which is presented to a lawmaking body for consideration.

Bill of Rights The first ten amendments to the Constitution.

civil liberties The rights and freedoms guaranteed to citizens in the Constitution and Bill of Rights.

constituent One of the citizens whom an elected official represents.

constitution A document containing the basic principles and laws of the nation or of a state.

curfew A regulation or ordinance requiring specified persons to vacate or not enter a particular area during named hours.

Federalist A person who favored a strong national government for the United States.

heresy An action or belief considered unacceptable by a dominant group.

judicial Related to the branch of government responsible for the justice system.

libel A false published statement that damages someone's reputation.

obscenity Something said, done, or depicted that is disgusting, repul-
sive, or morally unacceptable in a particular community.

petition An official request; to make an official request.

prosecute To bring legal action against an accused person or group.

quorum The minimum number of members authorized take action on
behalf of a group.

ratify To give formal approval.

sedition Conduct or language that incites rebellion against a
government.

slander A false spoken statement that damages someone's reputation.

suppression The act of stopping the publication or disclosure of
information.

Supreme Court The highest court in the judicial system of the
United States.

FOR MORE INFORMATION

American Civil Liberties Union (ACLU)
125 Broad Street, 18th Floor
New York, NY 10004
(212) 549-2500
Web site: http://www.aclu.org
The ACLU works in courts, legislatures, and committees to defend and preserve the individual rights and liberties that the Constitution and laws of the United States guarantee.

Americans United for Separation of Church and State
518 C Street NE
Washington, DC 20002
(202) 466-3234
Web site: http://www.au.org
This organization works on a wide range of pressing political and social issues in order to preserve the principle of church-state separation and protect religious freedom for all Americans.

Bill of Rights Institute
200 North Glebe Road, Suite 200
Arlington, VA 22203
(703) 894-1776
Web site: http://www.billofrightsinstitute.org
The Bill of Rights Institute is a nonprofit organization that educates young people about America's founding principles and liberties.

Canadian Civil Liberties Association

506-360 Bloor Street West
Toronto, ON M5S 1X1
Canada
(416) 363-0321
Web site: http://www.ccla.org
The Canadian Civil Liberties Association promotes respect for and observance of fundamental human rights and civil liberties through research, public education, law reform, and advocacy.

Department of Justice Canada

284 Wellington Street
Ottawa, ON K1A 0H8
Canada
(613) 957-4222
Web site: http://www.justice.gc.ca
Canada's Department of Justice works to ensure that Canada is a just and law-abiding nation with an accessible, efficient, and fair system of justice.

First Amendment Center

Vanderbilt University
1207 18th Avenue S
Nashville, TN 37212
(615) 727-1600
Web site: http://www.firstamendmentcenter.org
The First Amendment Center supports First Amendment freedoms through education, information, and entertainment. The center serves as a forum for the study and exploration of free expression issues, including freedom of speech, the press, religion, and the rights to assemble and petition the government.

Freedom Forum

555 Pennsylvania Avenue NW

Washington, DC 20001

(202) 292-6100

Web site: http://www.freedomforum.org

The Freedom Forum is a nonpartisan foundation that champions the First Amendment as a cornerstone of democracy.

Reporters Committee for Freedom of the Press

1101 Wilson Boulevard, Suite 1100

Arlington, VA 22209

(800) 336-4243

Web site: http://www.rcfp.org

This organization works to promote and defend the freedom of the press by providing advice, legal expertise, and legal assistance, especially to journalists.

Web Sites

Due to the changing nature of Internet links, Rosen Publishing has developed an online list of Web sites related to the subject of this book. This site is updated regularly. Please use this link to access the list:

http://www.rosenlinks.com/ausc/1st

FOR FURTHER READING

Boaz, John. *Free Speech* (Current Controversies). Farmington Hills, MI: Greenhaven Press, 2006.

Dougherty, Terri. *Freedom of Expression and the Internet* (Hot Topics). Detroit, MI: Lucent Books, 2010.

Edelman, Rob. *Freedom of the Press* (Issues on Trial). Farmington Hills, MI: Greenhaven Press, 2007.

Egendorf, Laura K. *Free Speech* (Compact Research). San Diego, CA: ReferencePoint Press, 2008.

Gibson, Karen Bush. *The Life and Times of John Peter Zenger* (Profiles in American History). Hockessin, DE: Mitchell Lane, 2007.

Gold, Susan Dudley. *Engel v. Vitale: Prayer in the Schools* (Supreme Court Milestones). Tarrytown, NY: Marshall Cavendish Benchmark, 2006.

Gold, Susan Dudley. *Tinker v. Des Moines: Free Speech for Students* (Supreme Court Milestones). Tarrytown, NY: Marshall Cavendish Benchmark, 2007.

McDonald, Joan Vos. *Religion and Free Speech Today: A Pro/Con Debate* (Issues in Focus Today). Berkeley Heights, NJ: Enslow Publishers, 2008.

Myers, Walter Dean. *The Cruisers*. New York, NY: Scholastic Press, 2010.

Slavicek, Louise Chipley. *Anne Hutchinson* (Leaders of the Colonial Era). Philadelphia, PA: Chelsea House, 2010.

Smith, Rich. *First Amendment: The Right of Expression*. Edina, MN: ABDO Publishing Company, 2008.

Steffens, Bradley. *Free Speech* (Ripped from the Headlines). Yankton, SD: Erickson Press, 2007.

BIBLIOGRAPHY

Abrams, Floyd. *Speaking Freely: Trials of the First Amendment*. New York, NY: Penguin Books, 2005.

Alderman, Ellen, and Caroline Kennedy. *In Our Defense: The Bill of Rights in Action*. New York, NY: William Morrow and Company, 1991.

Associated Press. "Student Gets Go-Ahead to Don Anti-Bush T-shirt." First Amendment Center, October 3, 2003. Retrieved December 21, 2009 (http://www.firstamendmentcenter.org/news.aspx?id=12020).

Belt, Gordon T. "Current Legislation & the First Amendment." First Amendment Center. Retrieved January 2, 2010 (http://www.first amendmentcenter.org/analysis.aspx?id=21598).

Belt, Gordon T. "The First Amendment in the Colonial Newspaper Press." First Amendment Center. Retrieved February 12, 2010 (http://www.firstamendmentcenter.org/about.aspx?item=colonial_press).

Buchanan, Brian J. "About the First Amendment." First Amendment Center. Retrieved January 14, 2010 (http://www.firstamendment center.org/about.aspx?item=about_firstamd).

Carlson-Thies, Stanley. "Freedom of Religion in American Public Life." Christian Leadership Alliance, February 19, 2010. Retrieved March 16, 2010 (http://christianleadershipalliance.org/articles/2010/freedomreligionlife.html).

Copeland, David A. *Debating the Issues in Colonial Newspapers: Primary Documents on the Events of the Period*. Westport, CT: Greenwood Press, 2000.

Darmer, M. Katherine B., Robert M. Baird, and Stuart E. Rosenbaum, eds. *Civil Liberties vs. National Security in a Post-9/11 World*. Amherst, NY: Prometheus Books, 2004.

Dautrich, Kenneth, David A. Yalof, and Mark Hugo López. *The Future of the First Amendment: The Digital Media, Civic Education, and Free Expression Rights in America's High Schools.* Lanham, MD: Rowman & Littlefield Publishers, 2008.

Finan, Christopher M. *From the Palmer Raids to the Patriot Act: A History of the Fight for Free Speech in America.* Boston, MA: Beacon Press, 2007.

First Amendment Center. "Religious Liberty in Public Life—Establishment Clause Overview." Retrieved January 17, 2010 (http://www.firstamendmentcenter.org/rel_liberty/establishment).

Haynes, Charles C. "Beyond the Shouting, What the Law Really Says About Religion." First Amendment Center, January 14, 2010. Retrieved January 14, 2010 (http://www.firstamendmentcenter.org/commentary.aspx?id=22497).

Hudson, David L., Jr. "Press—Libel & Defamation." First Amendment Center. Retrieved January 17, 2010 (http://www.firstamendmentcenter.org/press/topic.aspx?topic=libel_defamation).

Hudson, David L., Jr. "Student Expression in Speech—Cyberspeech." First Amendment Center, August 2008. Retrieved January 17, 2010 (http://www.firstamendmentcenter.org/speech/studentexpression/topic.aspx?topic=cyberspeech).

Hyneman, Charles S., and Donald S. Lutz. *American Political Writing During the Founding Era, 1760–1805*, Volume 1. Indianapolis, IN: Liberty Press, 1983.

Illinois First Amendment Center. "The History of the First Amendment." Retrieved November 7, 2009 (http://www.illinoisfirstamendmentcenter.com/history.php).

Labunski, Richard. *James Madison and the Struggle for the Bill of Rights* (Pivotal Moments in American History). New York, NY: Oxford University Press, 2006.

Lee, Douglas, and Bill Kenworthy. "Press—Shield Laws." First
    Amendment Center, August 2009. Retrieved January 17,
    2010 (http://www.firstamendmentcenter.org/press/topic.
    aspx?topic=shield_laws).

Legal Information Institute. "Supreme Court Collection: Topic:
    Freedom of Speech." Cornell University Law School. Retrieved
    January 11, 2010 (http://www.law.cornell.edu/supct/cases/topics/
    tog_freedom_of_speech.html).

Lief, Michael S., and H. Mitchell Caldwell. *And the Walls Came
    Tumbling Down: Closing Arguments That Changed the Way We Live—
    From Protecting Free Speech to Winning Women's Suffrage to Defending
    the Right to Die.* New York, NY: Scribner, 2004.

Lincoln University. "Freedom of Assembly." Retrieved January 2010
    (http://www.lincoln.edu/criminaljustice/hr/Assembly.htm).

Linder, Doug. "Introduction to the Free Speech Clause of the First
    Amendment." University of Missouri–Kansas City School of Law.
    Retrieved January 11, 2010 (http://www.law.umkc.edu/faculty/
    projects/ftrials/zenger/freespeech.htm).

Linder, Doug. "The Trial of John Peter Zenger: An Account." University
    of Missouri–Kansas City School of Law, 2001. Retrieved January 11,
    2010 (http://www.law.umkc.edu/faculty/projects/ftrials/zenger/
    zengeraccount.html).

Liptak, Adam. "Justices, 5–4, Reject Corporate Spending Limit." *New
    York Times,* January 21, 2010. Retrieved March 4, 2010 (http://www.
    nytimes.com/2010/01/22/us/politics/22scotus.html).

Litwin, Ethan E. "Investigative Reporters' Freedom and Responsibility:
    Reconciling Freedom of the Press with Privacy Rights." *Georgetown
    Law Journal,* February 1998. Retrieved March 8, 2010 (http://find
    articles.com/p/articles/mi_qa3805/is_199802/ai_n8805232).

Lively, Donald E. *Landmark Supreme Court Cases: A Reference Guide*. Westport, CT: Greenwood Press, 1999.

Mullally, Claire. "Religious Liberty in Public Life—Free Exercise Clause." First Amendment Center. Retrieved January 17, 2010 (http://www.firstamendmentcenter.org/rel_liberty/free_exercise).

Newton, Adam, and Bill Kenworthy. "Assembly—Curfews, Loitering & Freedom of Association." First Amendment Center, October 2006. Retrieved January 13, 2010 (http://www.firstamendmentcenter.org/assembly/topic.aspx?topic=freedom_association).

Newton, Adam, and Ronald K. L. Collins. "Petition—Overview." First Amendment Center. Retrieved January 17, 2010 (http://www.first amendmentcenter.org/petition/overview.aspx).

Ostrowski, James. "A Panoramic History of the First Amendment: Remarks to the Western New York Library Resources Council." March 22, 1995. Retrieved January 11, 2010 (http://apollo3.com/~jameso/first5.html).

Russell, Margaret M. *Freedom of Assembly and Petition: The First Amendment, Its Constitutional History, and the Contemporary Debate*. Amherst, NY: Prometheus Books, 2010.

School of Journalism & Mass Communication. "Journalism Ethics–Media Law–History of the Free Press." University of Wisconsin-Madison. Retrieved January 26, 2010 (http://www.journalismethics.ca/media_law/history_of_free_press.htm).

U.S. District Court for the Eastern District of Michigan. "Opinions—Judge Patrick J. Duggan." Retrieved July 19, 2010 (http://www.mied.uscourts.gov/Judges/archive/duggan.cfm).

Zacharias, Gary, and Jared Zacharias, eds. *The Bill of Rights* (At Issue in History). Farmington Hills, MI: Greenhaven Press/Thomson Gale, 2003.

INDEX

About the Author

Molly Jones is the author of three books, ten articles and stories for young readers, and several articles in professional journals. She has a Ph.D. in educational research and teaching certification in social studies and mathematics. Jones is a longtime community advocate for civil rights and civil liberties, and her current research and writing include contemporary and historical human rights issues, such as civil disobedience, euthanasia, and health care. She lives on Lake Murray near Columbia, South Carolina.

Photo Credits

Cover (left) Don Emmert/AFP/Getty Images; cover (middle) Michael Smith/ Getty Images; cover (right) Mark Wilson/Getty Images; p. 1 (top) www. istockphoto.com/Tom Nulens; p. 1 (bottom) www.istockphoto.com/Lee Pettet; p. 3 www.istockphoto.com/Nic Taylor; pp. 4–5 Bill Clark/Roll Call/Getty Images; p. 6 Rebecca Cook/Reuters/Landov; pp. 8, 18, 28, 39 © www. istockphoto.com/arturbo; pp. 9, 32–33 Hulton Archive/Getty Images; pp. 12–13, 17 © AP Images; p. 15 http://commons.wikimedia.org/wiki/File:Publick_ Occurrence_(page_1).jpg; pp. 20–21 Harry Hamburg/NY Daily News Archive via Getty Images; p. 22 SuperStock/Getty Images; pp. 26, 31 Library of Congress Prints and Photographs Division; p. 29 © Everett Collection/SuperStock; p. 36 Julian Wasser/Time & Life Pictures/Getty Images; pp. 40–41 Mike Simons/ Getty Images; pp. 44-45 Mark Abraham/Bloomberg via Getty Images; p. 49 James P. Blair/Newseum.

Editor: Andrea Sclarow; Photo Researcher: Amy Feinberg